I'M STILL STANDING

Empowering Stories of Faith and Resilience

DR. DONNA BOBO SPIVEY

STRIVE INTERNATIONAL
PUBLISHING

ISBN: 979-8-218-81698-8

Edit and Layout by Shonell Bacon

Publishing Coach: Telishia Berry

DEDICATION

This book is dedicated first to my Lord and Savior, Jesus Christ, the One who gave me strength to say "Yes" when life tried to silence me. To every woman, man, and child who has ever felt broken, abandoned, or unseen, may these words remind you that you are still standing because of the power inside you. And to my family, who have walked beside me through trials and triumphs, your love is a reflection of God's grace in my life. This is for you.

ACKNOWLEDGMENTS

I want to take this moment to acknowledge those who have been pillars of strength and encouragement throughout this journey. To my spiritual leaders and Apostle Regina Barefield Scott, thank you for speaking life into me and reminding me of the power of obedience. To my ministry family and intercessors, your prayers have carried me through valleys I could not have walked alone. To my dear friends, thank you for believing in the vision even before it was written on paper. And to my husband, children, grandchildren, mother, sister's and loved ones you are my constant inspiration. Finally, to every reader, thank you for opening your heart to my testimony. May this book impart faith, courage, and the boldness to say your own *yes* to God.

CONTENTS

INTRODUCTION

Life has a way of testing us in ways we never imagined. Storms arise, losses come, and disappointments leave marks that time alone cannot erase. Yet in the midst of it all, there is a voice within that whispers, *You are still standing.*

This anthology is a collection of voices from women who have endured trials, faced valleys, and walked through fire, yet emerged not destroyed but determined. Each story is a testimony of resilience, of grace, and of the power of a surrendered "Yes."

When we said, "Yes" to God, it was not always easy. That "Yes" cost us tears, courage, and trust beyond our own understanding. But it also birthed new strength, opened unexpected doors, and released healing in our lives. These pages carry more than words; they carry oil birthed out of brokenness, perseverance, and faith.

As you turn these pages, may you find yourself in these stories. May you feel hope rising again, courage awakening, and strength returning. Whether you are standing firm or struggling to rise, let this book remind you: **you are not alone, and you too can stand.**

This anthology is more than a book; it is a movement, a declaration, and a reminder that with God, *I'm Still Standing.*

*Your yes is more than a word.
It is an act of war that shakes
the gates of hell and opens the
doors of heaven.*

DR. DONNA BOBO SPIVEY

THE POWER OF MY YES

Choosing Obedience, Courage, and Faith over Fear

By Dr. Donna Bobo Spivey

There are moments in life that try to steal your footing. Storms that come without warning. Trials that shake you to the core. Losses, betrayals, disappointments, and battles you never asked for. And yet, when the dust settles, you discover a truth deeper than the pain: you are still standing.

I stand today not because life has been easy or because I was never knocked down, but because in the hardest seasons of my life, I gave God my yes. That yes became the anchor that held me when everything else seemed uncertain. It was not a one-time yes, but a daily surrender that gave me strength to rise, even when I wanted to quit.

The Cost of My Yes

Saying yes to God is never cheap. It demands trust when you don't understand the plan. It requires obedience when your flesh cries out for comfort. It calls for courage when fear whispers you're not enough.

There was a time when I thought my trials would silence me. I questioned if I had the strength to keep serving, keep leading, keep showing up. But each time I reached the end of myself, God invited me to simply say yes again. And every yes unlocked another measure of grace.

My yes did not eliminate the storms, but it gave me power to endure them. My yes did not silence the enemy's lies, but it gave me authority to stand on God's truth. My yes was the bridge between my brokenness and His wholeness.

The Women Who Said Yes

When I reflect on the Word of God, I see that history itself was shifted because women stood in agreement with God:

- Mary said yes to carrying Jesus, though it cost her reputation. Her surrender birthed salvation for the world.
- Esther said yes to risking her life, and through her courage, a nation was delivered.
- Deborah said yes to leading Israel, proving that when a woman stands in authority, battles are won.
- Hannah said yes through her prayer, and her son Samuel became a prophet to kings.
- The Woman at the Well said yes to truth, and her testimony ignited revival in an entire city.

Each yes was costly. Each yes required faith. Each yes left a legacy. And each yes reminds me that my agreement with God carries weight far beyond my own life.

The Power of Agreement

The Bible tells us in Amos 3:3, *"Can two walk together, except they be agreed?"* Agreement is the key to alignment. When I agree with God, I walk in step with His Spirit.

The enemy's greatest weapon is not always destruction—it is distraction. He wants us to say yes to fear, yes to shame, yes to silence. But when a woman says yes to God, she disrupts the enemy's plans and aligns herself with divine destiny.

Your yes is more than a word. It is an act of war. It is a declaration that you choose faith over fear, victory over defeat, and obedience over compromise. Your yes shakes the gates of hell and opens the doors of heaven.

Strengthened by My Yes

I look back at everything that should have broken me, and I realize—I am still standing. Not because I am strong in myself, but because each yes fortified me with supernatural strength.

I'm standing as a testimony. I'm standing as a voice. I'm standing as a vessel. And I want you to know that you can stand, too. Your trials do not define you. Your past does not silence you. Your scars do not disqualify you. If God is within you, you will not fall.

A Word to My Sisters

Woman of God, your yes is not small. It carries the power to shift your household, your church, your community, even your nation. Do not underestimate the sound of your agreement with heaven.

5

Say yes again, even if you are weary. Say yes again, even if you've failed. Say yes again, even if you feel overlooked. Every yes is building a foundation that the storms of life cannot destroy.

You are standing because God has need of your voice. You are standing because there are people attached to your obedience. You are standing because heaven has marked you for such a time as this.

PRAYER

Heavenly Father, Thank You for keeping me standing when life tried to knock me down. Thank You for the power of my yes. Today, I surrender again to Your will. Give me courage to speak when fear tells me to be silent. Give me strength to stand when trials press in around me. Let my yes carry weight, not only in my life, but in the lives of everyone I am called to touch. Align my heart with Yours, and let my voice release freedom, healing, and victory. In Jesus' name, Amen.

DECLARATION

- I declare that I am standing.
- I declare that the power of my yes shifts atmospheres.
- I declare that my agreement with God overrides the lies of the enemy.
- I declare that my voice carries authority, boldness, and purpose.
- I declare that I will not be silent, I will not back down, and I will not quit.
- I am rooted in grace, fueled by faith, and empowered by my yes.

REFLECTIONS FOR YOUR JOURNEY

1. What area of your life is God asking you to say yes to, even though it feels uncomfortable or costly?

2. How has one past yes to God shifted the course of your life or the lives of others?

_____

_____

_____

_____

_____

_____

_____

_____

_____

_____

_____

_____

_____

_____

_____

_____

ABOUT THE AUTHOR

Dr. Donna Spivey, founder of Donna Spivey Ministries, is a dynamic preacher, teacher, and author. Through her vision I'm Still Standing, she empowers women to rise from trials with resilience, faith, and purpose. Her ministry inspires transformation, healing, and strength to stand firmly in God's truth.

I stand bold, unshaken, and free, with a spirit that soars.

◆———————————◆

DR. AQUANETTA DAVIS

BULLETPROOF IN FAITH

A Testimony of Unshakable Resilience

By Dr. Aquanetta Davis

I stand bold, unshaken, and free, with a spirit that soars. I'm not stuck, I'm unstoppable—breathing life and freedom. I'm empowered by God's strength and love, unchained and unbound. I'm fearfully and wonderfully made—a prophet, mother, overcomer, demon slayer, and daughter of Jesus Christ. I walk in confidence, unapologetic and unafraid, with a heart that beats strong and a voice that speaks truth. I'm anointed with God's presence and guidance, blessed with gratitude and humility, courageous in standing up for what I believe in, and hopeful in the midst of uncertainty and doubt. I am Miracles, Signs, and Wonders. I am Dr. Davis, and I AM BULLETPROOF. "Put on the full armor of God, so that when the day of evil comes, you may be able to stand your ground, and after you have done everything, to stand" (Ephesians 6:13).

Unwavering Love, Unshakeable Faith

It often amazes me how I'm still standing strong, despite a childhood marked by impulsivity and a touch of chaos. As a child, I was very witty, and I had an overwhelming urge to care for my mother and grandmother—two remarkable women who epitomized grace and strength. Their unwavering love and wisdom always reminded me of the greatness within myself. Being a part of the vibrant Los Angeles faith community, I was blessed to be involved with Bishop Blake at West Angeles, Bishop MacMurray at Greater Bethany Missionary, and Goodwill Baptist Church. With God woven into the fabric of my soul, I always felt I had my heart secure in His hands.

But I will sing of your strength, in the morning I will sing of your love; for you are my fortress, my refuge in times of trouble.

Psalm 59:16

The Love & Innocence of My Youth

As I grew older, I often pondered, *Why is God so incredibly good to me?* I can't recall a time when I truly lacked anything. Even if I faced challenges, I remained clueless. My life felt like a beautiful tapestry of two experiences. With my mother in West L.A., life was filled with laughter, peace, and love. She ensured my sister and I would thrive creatively in various programs. Then, there was South Central and my grandmother, the epitome of elegance and intelligence. She taught us the value of hard work, a dollar, and resilience. Despite the trials surrounding her, she stood tall, unfazed. I now recognize that joy, peace, and happiness were the constants in my life, and yes, it might sound cliché, but that is my truth. I love being alive; I adore God.

Even though I was a bit naive and it sometimes led to questionable choices, it also allowed my heart to love without boundaries. I dove headfirst into the depths of love, embracing its beauty and imperfections. Reflecting on my journey, I've come to realize that love is a language of my soul—one that communicates, "I care about you, I value you, and I'm here for you." It speaks in vulnerability, empathy, and understanding. When we nurture this language, we build unshakeable bridges of love that can withstand life's trials.

From Challenges to Strength: My Bulletproof Journey

As I mentioned before, life's challenges never truly brought me down because I am a dreamer at heart. I recall moments when the burdens seemed unbearable, suffocating me. I felt death, but I couldn't die. I've faced the unimaginable—surviving a drive-by shooting with five bullets piercing my body and being resuscitated multiple times. I realized God says, "Tell them I AM" (Exodus 3:14). For me, this means standing on His Word. Love enfolds many emotions, and I've realized we decide how to respond in love during our situations—just as the Scriptures state, "Love is patient, love is kind…" (1 Corinthians 13:4). Hallelujah, I stand as a living miracle, echoing God's grace and favor. When all seemed lost, He reminded me, "I'm still with you, I'm still holding onto you." I found strength in His promise: "I can do all things through Christ that strengthens me" (Psalms 4:13). I've experienced pain, but I've learned to rise above it. I've chosen to respond with love. I am a living testimony that I AM BULLETPROOF.

Still Standing, Still Growin'

My mother's and grandmother's words weren't just advice—they were a blueprint for living. They taught me how to stand firm and walk in my **PRETTY**. This journey hasn't been easy; I've walked in celibacy, loneliness, and feelings of abandonment, doing it all God's way and trying to leave worldly desires behind to stay holy. I have stood firm in God's love and promises even when He would tell me He's coming to take one of my loved ones. **Lord**…that might seem unreal to some, but I said what I said. **I am cried out**. I walk in victory. I am a living testament to God's goodness and mercy. As I reflect on the person I am today, I am reminded that this legacy did not stop with me. I've carried those lessons to my own children. The truth is this legacy grows one generation at a time.

Train up a child in the way he should go, and when he is old, he will not depart from it.

Proverbs 22:6

Twice Loved: A Story of Marriage, Lessons, and Growth

Having had the privilege of being married to two incredible men, one a profound love and the other a love on a beautiful journey, each relationship taught me invaluable lessons about love, sacrifice, and the complexities of human connections. One key reason I'm still standing is that I've learned to navigate the challenges of marriage with an open heart and a willingness to grow. Loving someone unconditionally unveils the truth that while love is essential, it requires understanding, patience, and forgiveness.

Rooted in Love: A Testament to Standing Strong

So, how am I still standing after all the challenges I've faced? I'm standing because I've learned to love without conditions, to forgive without forgetting, and to trust without guarantees. I'm standing because I've discovered that love is a choice, and it's a choice that I make every day. I'm standing because I've learned to speak the language of love, and it's a language that has transformed my life in ways I never thought possible. It's this blend of resilience, faith, hope, and love that anchors me firmly in life's beautiful journey.

I Am Miracles, Signs, and Wonders.

I AM Dr. Aquanetta Davis.

And now these three remain: faith, hope, and love. But the greatest of these is love.

1 Corinthians 13:13

REFLECTIONS FOR YOUR JOURNEY

1. What moments in your life revealed that you are "bulletproof" in faith?

2. How can choosing love daily help you stand firm in times of trials?

_____

_____

_____

_____

_____

_____

_____

_____

_____

_____

_____

_____

_____

_____

_____

_____

ABOUT THE AUTHOR

Dr. Aquanetta Davis is a mother, pastor, prophet, and servant of God, anointed at the age of 5. She founded Skindeep Bulletproof Outreach and P.R.E.T.T.Y.* Ministries with 35+ years of ministry knowledge. She is a college graduate and holds a (ThD) and an honorary (DD) degree, along with a strong commitment to community service. *P.R.E.T.T.Y. stands for **P**erfecting **R**oyalty **E**difying **T**rue **T**estimony in **Y**ou.

Instagram: Skindeepdrd43 | Facebook: Aquanetta Davis

Forgiveness is not weakness. It is strength. It is the bridge from pain to purpose.

DR. CYNTHIA DIVINITY

GRACE TO RISE:

From Forgiveness to Freedom

By Dr. Cynthia Divinity

Have you ever had a season where you didn't know what tomorrow would look like… if you would make it through the day?

I have. My marriage ended in betrayal. I grieved the loss of a child I never got to meet. My career, 18 years of dedication, was threatened by false allegations. One morning, after a sleepless night, I walked outside to leave for work only to find my car had been stolen. I called in, devastated, only to be ordered to come in anyway. Later, I learned why: his mistress had called my job, making false accusations tied to his arrest.

There I was—car gone, marriage broken, name dragged through the mud, career hanging by a thread. I was isolated, broken, uncertain, feeling worthless, abandoned, and forgotten. And yet, in the midst of that pain, I heard God whisper: "I've got you. My grace is sufficient."

It was in that valley I realized forgiveness wasn't just about others. Forgiveness is about freedom. It is about releasing anger, bitterness, and resentment, even when apologies never come. It is about letting God's grace flow through you so that your future is not held hostage by the past.

I surrendered my struggles to God—praying, fasting, pouring out my heart until I was physically weak but spiritually strong. Through that surrender, God's grace opened doors: mentors appeared, opportunities arrived, and what felt like the end became the start of my purpose. Forgiveness became freedom, and my darkest season transformed into my greatest blessing.

Forgiveness as Grace

Forgiveness is a choice, not a feeling. It is an act of faith. Often, we hold on to past hurts because we feel justified in our anger, or we believe the other person owes us an apology. But God's grace teaches us otherwise. Just as He restored me in my brokenness, He calls us to restore others through forgiveness.

As Colossians 3:13 reminds us, *"Bear with each other and forgive one another if any of you has a grievance against someone. Forgive as the Lord forgave you."*

Scripture also teaches in Matthew 6:14-15, *"For if you forgive other people when they sin against you, your heavenly Father will also forgive you. But if you do not forgive others their sins, your Father will not forgive your sins."*

We are not called to hold grudges. We are called to release. We are not called to stay in the valley. We are called to rise. Forgiveness is not weakness. It is strength. It is the bridge from pain to purpose. It allows us to move forward without the weight of resentment. And it creates space for God to bless us beyond what we could imagine.

The GRACE That Carried Me

- **G– God's Gift**: Grace is freely given, not earned (Ephesians 2:8).
- **R– Renewal**: Grace gives us a fresh start each day (Lamentations 3:22-23).
- **A– Alignment**: Grace steadies our steps and aligns us with God's will (Proverbs 3:5-6).
- **C– Courage**: Grace empowers us to forgive, rise, and step into the unknown (Joshua 1:9).
- **E– Elevation**: Grace lifts us above pain into purpose (James 4:10).

The Power of Letting Go

One of the greatest lessons I learned is that forgiveness is not conditional. You don't have to wait for an apology to be whole. You don't have to wait for others to change to reclaim your peace. You let go because God's grace has already restored you. Holding on only prolongs your pain.

By forgiving, I freed myself from the prison of bitterness. I opened my hands to receive the blessings God had already prepared. My darkest season—the betrayal, the loss, the lies—was actually my biggest blessing.

Scriptural Anchors

The Bible is full of people who had to start over:

- Job lost everything, but God restored him.
- Joseph was betrayed, imprisoned, and forgotten, yet God raised him to leadership.
- Peter denied Christ, but grace restored him, and he became a pillar of the church.

Like them—and like me—you may have to start over, but with God, starting over is not a setback. It's a setup to rise with dignity, walk in purpose, and forgive as you have been forgiven.

The Strategy to Rise
- **Surrender**– Let go and let God take control.
- **Seek**– Pray, fast, and ask God for direction.
- **Silence**– Remove the noise, distractions, and voices that don't serve your healing.
- **Stand**– Even when weak, stand on the Word of God.
- **Step**– Don't wait until you feel ready; take the next step, and God meets you there.

Psalm 30:5 reminds us, *"Weeping may endure for a night, but joy comes in the morning."*

Reflections

Your past does not disqualify you. Your mistakes do not define you. Your losses are not the end of your story. You may have been knocked down, betrayed, or overlooked, but you will rise. Rise in grace. Rise in strength. Rise in forgiveness.

When you rise in grace, forgive as you've been forgiven, and embrace God's plan, you free yourself and make room for God to move through you—guiding, strengthening, and aligning you with purpose beyond imagination.

I've been broken, betrayed, and buried under grief, but by God's grace, I'm still standing. Not just standing—I'm stronger, freer, and ready to rise into everything He has called me to be.

Jeremiah 29:11 reminds us: *"For I know the plans I have for you,"* declares the Lord, *"plans to prosper you and not to harm you, plans to give you hope and a future."*

REFLECTIONS FOR YOUR JOURNEY

1. What is one area of your life where you are still holding onto hurt, and how would releasing it free you to step into your purpose?

2. How has God's grace shown up in your darkest seasons? What did you learn about yourself in the process?

_____

_____

_____

_____

_____

_____

_____

_____

_____

_____

_____

_____

_____

_____

_____

_____

ABOUT THE AUTHOR

Cynthia Divinity is a dynamic entrepreneur and community leader with over 25 years of service in business development and advocacy. Her career began in law enforcement, where she served 18 years before founding Divine Employment Services in 2017. Dedicated to empowering adults with intellectual and developmental disabilities, she expanded her mission through Divine Inclusions, offering programs that promote independence, wellness, and community integration across Southern California. In 2020, Cynthia launched Beautifully "BU" Unveiled and The Women's Empowerment Group, guiding young women into womanhood and fostering lifelong community and sisterhood. Passionate about impact, Cynthia continues creating opportunities for growth and empowerment.

From that moment, I made a choice: I would arise and fight for myself and for my children. The tears dried up, and my mind shifted into battle mode.

PASTOR TYLESHA JONES

ARISE AND FIGHT

A Teen Mother's Journey Through Loss, Prayer, and Spiritual Warfare to Bring Her Children Home

By Pastor Tylesha Jones

A Shattered Beginning

"Arise and fight" is a command issued by the Commander of all commanders, God Almighty Himself. I heard this command the day my world was shattered. I was only sixteen years old when my second child stopped breathing in my arms while I was feeding her. Born prematurely at just one pound and nine ounces, she struggled to survive from the very beginning. That day, I noticed she had stopped moving. Not a sound came from her tiny body. When I tried to remove the bottle from her mouth, her gums had clamped down on the nipple. Her lips were bluish in color. Fear and panic overwhelmed me.

I immediately called 911. When paramedics arrived, they opened her airway and placed a trachea in her throat. I stood in shock as they worked to save her life.

Within a week, things got worse. Police officers and social services showed up at my home to perform a welfare check on my oldest daughter, who was just two years old. They told me they had to remove her from my care. I screamed as I held my daughter tightly, pressing my body against the wall, trying to keep them from taking her. But the officer pulled her from my arms. At only sixteen, I stood there shattered once again.

Learning to Fight

If I had never experienced a battle before, this was certainly one. It felt like the enemy had landed a blow so hard it knocked the breath out of me. Hopelessness filled my mind, and all I wanted to do was hide and cry.

I crawled into my mother's old station wagon, hoping no one would find me. But God knew exactly where I was. After some time, I heard the car door open. It was my brother. "Tylesha, Mama is calling you," he said gently.

I mustered the strength to go inside. My mother sat me down and, with tender yet strong words, said, "God wants you to rise up and fight."

She explained that this was not a physical battle but a spiritual one. She taught me that prayer was a weapon. She reminded me that I had an enemy named Satan, who would not just sit back and allow me to fight for my children. I had to stand on God's Word and trust that He was with me. From that moment, I made a choice: I would arise and fight for myself and for my children. The tears dried up, and my mind shifted into battle mode.

Spiritual Warfare

Prayer and the Word of God became my weapons. *"The weapons of our warfare are not carnal, but mighty through God to the pulling down of strongholds"* (2 Corinthians 10:4) became my anchor. I realized that if I wanted victory, I had to shift from defeat in my mind to the position of a winner. I began to declare: *"Greater is He that is in me than he that is in the world."*

I didn't just read the Word—I studied it, meditated on it, and spoke it in prayer. The Word of God became my sword in the battle Satan waged against me.

I also surrounded myself with believers who stood on God's Word. I joined a Bible-believing ministry and pursued God with all my heart. What I didn't realize was that while I was pursuing God, He was pursuing me with His love and kindness.

Every time I entered His presence in prayer, my heart overflowed with love, tears flowed, and my asking turned into thanksgiving.

Surrendered Faith

In prayer, something shifted. I no longer said, "My children." Instead, I said, "Your children." I realized they belonged to God, not me. My faith was strengthened in knowing that we were all in His hands. Over time, God brought my children home. He proved Himself faithful and true. I now praise Him because He taught me how to win battles through prayer. I declare today that I know Him as faithful not because the road was easy, but because I endured the process.

REFLECTIONS FOR YOUR JOURNEY

1. What battles in your life require you to "arise and fight" in prayer?
2. In what ways can you shift from a defeated mindset to the mindset of a victor?

_____

_____

_____

_____

_____

_____

_____

_____

_____

_____

_____

_____

_____

_____

About the Author

Associate Pastor Tylesha Adaeze Jones is under the leadership of Apostle and Pastor Josephine Odinigwe of Miracle Christian Center, where she is the prayer coordinator of the ministry. Committed to a lifestyle of prayer and the word of God, Pastor Tylesha is a true servant in God's Kingdom.

I am living proof that pain can lead to power and tragedy can turn into testimony.

DR. MELVORA E. MOORE-FULTON

TRUSTING IN THE UNKNOWN

A Journey of Faith, Healing, and God's Sustaining Power

By Dr. Melvora E. Moore-Fulton

Life challenges come and go in everyone's life. Life happens when things don't go the way you plan them. We all have moments when we sit back and ask, "Why, Lord?" I know that question well. It has echoed in my heart since I was a little girl.

For me, the answer comes when I look back over my life and see that, through every storm, every heartbreak, every trial—I'm still standing.

A Childhood of Loss

My story began with loss. When I was just ten years old, I lost my mother. Ten years old, still a child, still needing hugs, bedtime prayers, and words of encouragement. That day, everything changed. Suddenly, my siblings and I had to grow up faster than we ever should have.

I remember sitting on my bed, crying, whispering into the dark, "Why my mother, God? Why take her?" I didn't understand. I felt lost. I felt unloved. I felt confused about my future.

Psalm 34:18 says, *"The Lord is close to the brokenhearted and saves those who are crushed in spirit."* At the time, I didn't yet grasp how true that was. But God was near even when I couldn't feel Him. He sent people to step in and hold me up when I wanted to fall apart. He sent teachers who cared, neighbors who helped, and most importantly, He gave me the church.

The church became my refuge. Sunday mornings became my lifeline. The choir became my safe place, where I could sing my way through pain. The sermons reminded me that even though I had lost my mother, I had a heavenly Father who promised never to leave me or forsake me.

Isaiah 41:10 says, *"Fear not, for I am with you; be not dismayed, for I am your God. I will strengthen you, I will help you, I will uphold you with my righteous right hand."* Slowly but surely, those words began to sink in.

A Calling to Teach

Still, the journey wasn't easy. Grief has a way of lingering. There were moments in my teenage years when I felt invisible, as if no one understood the hurt I carried. I had to learn that healing is a process, not an event. God was teaching me patience, faith, and endurance. Even then, He was preparing me for something greater.

In the 1970s, I saw a dream come true. I graduated from college with a degree in education. At first, it seemed impossible that I would ever become a teacher, but God opened the door.

I taught students from many different backgrounds and nationalities. My classroom was a place of diversity, discovery, and growth. I soon learned that children are unique little people, each with their own personality and story.

As a teacher, I thought I was there to teach them, but in many ways, they were teaching me. They taught me patience, compassion, creativity, and how to see the world through their eyes.

After forty-two years of teaching, I retired, grateful for the journey. Teaching was more than a career; it was a calling. Spending my life with "God's little people," as I often called them, was one of the greatest blessings of my life. And even through the challenges of the classroom, I am still standing.

A Battle for Life

As I grew into adulthood, new challenges came my way. I faced trials that shook my faith and forced me to trust God on a deeper level. One of the hardest seasons was when I went into a diabetic coma.

I was unaware of what was happening to my body. One moment I felt weak, the next everything went dark. For four long days, my family waited and prayed. Doctors didn't know what the outcome would be. But heaven heard every prayer, and by the grace of God, I woke up.

When I opened my eyes, I knew I had been given a second chance at life. My faith was no longer just something I talked about. It became the anchor that held me.

Philippians 4:13 became my anthem: *"I can do all things through Christ who strengthens me."* I held onto that scripture through every doctor's visit, every adjustment to my new reality, every fear that tried to creep in.

That experience changed me. It made me determined not just to survive but to thrive. I decided that if God had spared me, there must be a purpose for my life, and I was going to find it.

A Vision for Purpose

That's when the vision for my future became clear. I opened group home facilities to provide care and a safe environment for those who needed it most.

The very thing I longed for as a grieving child, a place of stability, love, and protection, I was now able to create for others.

Romans 8:28 reminds us, *"And we know that all things work together for good to those who love God, to those who are called according to His purpose."*

Losing my mother was painful, but it taught me compassion. The coma was terrifying, but it gave me clarity. Every challenge that once made me cry became a stepping stone to something greater.

A Declaration of Faith

Now, when I say, "I'm still standing," it's not just words; it's a declaration. I'm standing because God carried me through grief. I'm standing because He woke me up from that coma and said, "Your story isn't over."

I'm standing because my trials taught me to trust Him even when I can't trace Him. And I stand before you today to tell you that if He did it for me, He can do it for you.

If you are walking through a season of loss, if you are facing sickness, if you are questioning God, wondering if He hears you, hold on. Your story is not over.

Psalm 30:5 says, *"Weeping may endure for a night, but joy comes in the morning."*

Your morning is coming. You may feel like you are barely hanging on but know that God is closer than you think. He has a plan, even in the pain.

So today, I declare I am still standing. Not because life has been easy, but because God has been faithful. I am still standing because grace picked me up, mercy kept me, and love restored me.

If you are in a valley right now, know that you are not alone. The same God who strengthened me will strengthen you. The same God who gave me purpose will give you purpose too.

I am living proof that pain can lead to power. I am living proof that faith can turn tragedy into testimony. I am living proof that with God, you can survive anything and not just survive but thrive. I'm still standing, and with God's help, so will you.

REFLECTIONS FOR YOUR JOURNEY

1. When have you had to trust God even when you could not see the outcome?

2. How can your own pain be transformed into purpose for helping others?

_____

_____

_____

_____

_____

_____

_____

_____

_____

_____

_____

_____

_____

_____

_____

_____

ABOUT THE AUTHOR

Dr. Melvora E Moore-Fulton is an author, conference speaker, pastor, CEO of several non-profits, and teacher with over 40 years of experience working with adults and children with special needs. More important than all of these things, she is a wife, mother, and servant of God.

Facebook: Melvora MooreFulton

We are not defined by circumstance but transformed by purpose.

ANDREA MYLES

STANDING THROUGH THE STORM

Finding Resilience, Healing, and Strength in God

By Andrea Myles

Dense clouds filled the night sky as the moon pierced the darkness and cast a sheer silhouette down the narrow corridor. The patter of my heels echoed through the silence as I rushed past the tall panels, crystal sideboards, quartz countertops, marble flooring, and pristine chandeliers.

How could I be living the dream, only to wake up in a nightmare? I grabbed my purse and keys from the cascading staircase framed with pictures of what everyone saw, what everyone expected—a perfect family. A power couple, corporate executive, pastor, and his family etched in 25 years of still frames that could only capture what was.

I took a deep breath and could feel the rush of adrenaline, uncertainty, compounding pressure, expectation almost imploding before I could turn the keys to lock the front door. *Am I making the biggest mistake of my life?*

It was 4 a.m., and my next two-and-a-half-hour commute through rush hour traffic in the city would become the battleground where I wrestled with shame, argued with the coffin of displaced stigma, and confronted the risk of stepping forward into a future I had never prepared for.

I practiced holding my emotions to conceal the anxiety of what's next. As I closed the car door, the quiet neighborhood—well-manicured yards, luxury cars in the driveways—served as a mask hiding pain I could no longer bear.

I drove past the fountains and headed toward the freeway. Everything was safe in the car; there were no stares of judgment, gossip, or ridicule. Like a vault of secrets locked in a safe deposit box, I opened an inner dialogue between my heart and spirit. *I'm now in a free space. I can talk.*

Get Up!

"Get up, girl. You've got to stand!"

It was my first day after confirming my worst fear. My knees were buckling. The complacency of my present state conditioned a fear of not knowing how to pick up the pieces. Pieces of my identity. Pieces of my children. Pieces of my life.

Tears began to rush down my face as memories accelerated uncovered emotions. I had to let go.

I was safe to unpack everything here—in the vault of my commute. One loud sigh of pent-up emotions filled the car with cries of agony as I saw my life in the rearview mirror. *We built this family together.*

Each mile of the commute unfolded the aftermath of infidelity with remnants of hurt and mistrust. I recalled the prayers of solace and the gut-wrenching intuition confirmed by the discovery of his five-year secret relationship.

I journeyed through the children we had, the careers we achieved, the lives we touched. Everyone might not agree with my choice, but that day, I chose to stand.

I chose to no longer operate from a deficit at the expense of depositing into the emotional accounts of others. I needed to file a Chapter 7 bankruptcy of self-worth, bankruptcy of peace, and bankruptcy of a love that was once reciprocal. But that day, I was closing the accounts.

I unlocked the vault of every thought and screamed with a loud shriek of pain. I was free here. I'm sure I must be on someone's camera roll, finally that "crazy woman" spotted along the highway. But in that moment, I was free by undeniable truth, self-love, and unwavering resolve to build again.

I could never choose to stay in an image of hypocrisy and suffer the demise of authenticity. In this vault, I discovered wisdom, perseverance, and treasures that empowered me to stand.

This Won't Knock You Down!

"You will stand through this."

The dialogue between my heart and mind continued. I cleaved to memories of growing up in South L.A. and the resilience that came from experiences like grocery shopping only to discover the wheels of the cart locked at the edge of the parking lot. That day, my sister and I walked blocks with wrists warped by the strain of plastic bags filled with heavy groceries. We learned how to keep going.

I remembered riding the bus to adult school and hearing the shatter of the back window pierced by a stray bullet. Still, I was willing to ride through the trenches to get my GED.

I held onto the mindset I developed while serving overseas in the military as one of the first women integrated on a foreign deployed ship. I learned to keep going.

After receiving a GED, I took the next steps to a high school diploma and an undergraduate degree in accounting, followed by a master's in business.

This won't knock me down.

I had already learned to emerge from the ashes of sexual assault, the uncertainty of living in a hotel, the hospital stays, and the grief. I had learned to stand once before, and this would not knock me down.

Though your hurt may be recent and your tragedy may be great, you can stand. This won't knock you down.

Be Still

I had to learn to be still. I carried Psalm 46:10, *"Be still and know that I am God,"* close to my heart. I found a sense of being as I released the constant sense of doing.

My days were filled with appointments, schedules, and priorities. I recall depleted days when physical or emotional recovery was impossible through the busyness of doing, whether it was trips, entertainment, money, or shopping.

My recovery came from being still. The more still I became, the more of God I came to know. I rushed into the arms of Christ, my Savior, who came to rescue me.

One day, while standing in my closet, I tried to quickly hide my tears as my daughter walked into the room. As I wiped my eyes, I heard His voice say: *"Allow them to see you cry. Hiding your pain will only normalize burying your hurt. You may want your children to see your strength, but this will unintentionally cause them to question their own hurt and minimize the trauma in young girls processing the grief of letting go."*

So I stood still and held my girls through our hurt.

I stood still in the grace to resist the temptation of running to a title, a career, or a new relationship to heal inner pain.

I stood still in faith with a healthy community, vulnerable in my identity hidden in Christ.

I stood still with a groundbreaking truth of internal affirmation, and I went from being to becoming.

Your Next Chapter

"Your current page looks nothing like your next chapter."

I reminded myself of the grace to accept a future I had not yet experienced by taking the present time to heal.

I was done running. I would no longer run from the pain of divorce or the shame of not aligning with societal norms. I couldn't run into the paralyzing grips of history because I was uncomfortable walking into a new future.

But I had to learn to walk. Walk into healing. Walk into restoration. Walk into forgiveness—and be restored.

I embraced my next chapter, a chapter of empathy for my ex-husband and liberating peace.

We are not defined by circumstance but transformed by purpose. The vault is open, and I'm still standing!

REFLECTIONS FOR YOUR JOURNEY

1. What "vault" moments in your life have allowed you to release pain and find freedom?

2. How can standing still in God's presence help you prepare for your next chapter?

_____

_____

_____

_____

_____

_____

_____

_____

_____

_____

_____

_____

_____

_____

_____

_____

ABOUT THE AUTHOR

Andrea Myles is a trailblazing preacher, financial expert, and U.S. Navy veteran who rose from humble beginnings in South Central Los Angeles to become a Regional CFO and corporate executive. With over 25 years in federal service, she oversees a $3 billion portfolio and mentors emerging leaders nationwide. A nationally recognized award-winner, her story of perseverance, leadership, and impact inspires readers to rise above challenges and lead with purpose. Passionate about empowering others, especially women and youth, Ms. Myles writes to uplift, motivate, and ignite the next generation.

What if I had given up? I can think of countless times when most people would have, but God kept me.

TEROLYN PHINSEE

No Option to Quit

The Faith That Carried Me Through

By Terolyn Phinsee

Quitting is an option for everyone. However, I refuse to allow quitting to be an option for me.

As I reflect on my life's journey, I can think of the countless times that I wanted to give up. As a young single mother who left an abusive relationship while in my second year of college, I was determined not to be a statistic. I had a vision for me and my daughter.

I would take the bus each morning in the dark, before the sun arose, with my 1-year-old daughter to daycare, and get on the next bus to get to work. Often asleep for the majority of the bus ride, my daughter would wake up immediately as I kissed her cheek and signed her into the daycare.

The days were long, and my tasks at work were arduous, yet I was grateful to have a government job with great benefits. I would clock out at 4:30 p.m. sharp, to ensure that I did not miss the bus and could make it to Long Beach Day Nursery on time to avoid a late fee. The daycare provided subsidized funding to keep my childcare costs down, so following all of the rules was critical.

Pushing Forward

I established a goal—to pick my daughter up from the nursery and walk one mile, then attend Long Beach City College to take night classes toward an Associate of Science degree in the School of Business, Computer Information Systems.

Most of my professors were very considerate of me. Some were skeptical; however, they agreed that I could take my daughter to class as long as she did not cry and disturb the other students.

My days became longer: up at 5 am for our daycare and work journey, then straight to night classes after work as my daughter slept in her stroller, and finally catching the bus to get home at night by 10 p.m. The routine was repeated daily.

In the second week of my daughter being at the daycare and my first week of college, I got off the bus, took my daughter into the nursery, and was greeted by the supervisor. She informed me that if my daughter continued to cry all day, she would not be able to stay.

I wanted to quit. I knew my family couldn't babysit for me. I cried; I was a new Christian and didn't yet live a life that glorified God. I committed to honoring God with my life, and God showed me and my precious daughter His grace and mercy.

An Angel in Disguise

There was Marie, a beautiful older African American Christian woman working in the kitchen at the nursery. Each day, my daughter would cry, grabbing Marie's apron string and following her around. Marie would comfort her and hold her.

I believe Marie was our guardian angel. She made it a point to come to work extra early, cook the meals for the children, so she could spend time with my precious 1-year-old. Within days, the crying stopped, and the supervisor assured me that I could bring my daughter to daycare.

What if I had given up? I can think of countless times when most people would have, but God kept me, my daughters, grandchildren, and my family overall.

Standing on the Word

I stand on Psalm 84:11: *"For the LORD God is a sun and shield; the LORD bestows favor and honor; no good thing does he withhold from those whose walk is blameless."*

I am far from being perfect. Yet, I know that while I was yet in sin, Christ died for me.

I am still standing because of the promises of God in His Word to keep me and my family. No matter where you find yourself, get up and say what Micah 7:8 says: *"Do not gloat over me, my enemy! Though I have fallen, I will rise. Though I sit in darkness, the LORD will be my light."*

My Testimony

I finished college and received my AS in Computer Programming. I married, have two beautiful daughters—both college graduates—and two amazing grandsons. Together, we love the Lord!

We are all going to make mistakes in this life. You must not quit. Get up, repent, forgive, apologize, seek God's wisdom, the guidance of the Holy Spirit, and demonstrate the fruit of the Spirit.

And when you have done all to stand, stand therefore, with your body girded about in truth. **STAND in God's strength.**

REFLECTIONS FOR YOUR JOURNEY

1. What situation in your life once made you want to quit, but God gave you the strength to rise again?

2. Who has been a "Marie" in your life, someone God sent to help carry you through?

_____

_____

_____

_____

_____

_____

_____

_____

_____

_____

_____

_____

_____

_____

_____

About the Author

Terolyn Phinsee is a senior software compliance manager. She is certified as an IT software asset manager with the IAITAM, Microsoft Office User Specialist certified, Certified HIPAA Security Specialist, and the former president of IAMCP (International Association Microsoft Channel Partners). Terolyn is the program director for Titus STEAM Preparatory, a community-based 501c3 organization providing technical training to inner-city underserved youth. She is the CEO of Zip & Go Assist, a technology consulting company based in Los Angeles, CA. She will complete her Theology MBA in June 2026.

God was there all the time. He woke me up and helped me regather the fragmented parts of my life.

◆————————————————◆

ROSALYN COURTNEY RICHARDSON

THE REGATHERING

Finding Strength, Healing, and Purpose in Brokenness

By Rosalyn Courtney Richardson

Who Dropped You?

The year was 1968. All eyes were on me as I took my turn to drop the glass globe which housed my mom's clock. My brother had already dropped it, and it did not break. I was nervous, but I dropped it anyway. It crashed onto the carpeted floor and shattered into pieces. As they pointed their fingers, I stooped down to gather the larger pieces. I cut my finger and was now bleeding and crying. I cried myself to sleep. Mom awakened me out of my sleep. No one came to my rescue. I was on my own.

Pick Up the Pieces

I quickly realized that it is impossible to pick up the small pieces without help or guidance. It started to fall apart around 2008. It had been three years since I'd married my God-given mate. We were introduced by my son-in-law. He wanted his dad to have a good wife. From the very beginning, I was interrogated.

We were at my future in-laws' home. My introduction was met with, "Can I ask you something?"

I said, "Sure."

"Are you crazy?" his daughter asked.

"No, but most crazy people say that."

She then went on to ask, "What are your intentions with my father?"

I answered, "You should ask your father what his intentions are with me. I'm single by choice."

That caused a pause, as I stood my ground. My husband held my hand as we faced the firing squad. I didn't realize I was glimpsing into my future. The blatant statements of disrespect. One said, "I don't have anything against you. I just don't want my father to marry anybody."

Often, my husband brought corrections, but they went unheeded. The many attacks against our marriage weren't just from his family, but also his disapproving friends with their religious ideologies about remarriage. I also had to deal with a misguided ex-wife who would show up wherever we were. Every time we would gather together in my home for what seemed to be a good time, something would inevitably explode.

My mantra at the time was, *I don't make other people's issues my issues.* But there were so many issues.

A Barrage of Trials

It was during those years that my husband became caregiver to his disabled niece, then later his brother and both parents. My youngest daughter, who was the only minor child in our union, felt betrayed because of the many times my husband and I were dishonored and disrespected while still opening our hearts and our doors. She couldn't see that I was committed to honoring God. My acceptance of them felt like a rejection of her.

I had so many restless nights. I would play worship CDs on repeat all night. I was trying to do a balancing act in the midst of carrying a broken spirit. I was often unfocused but still operating in all phases of life. I would take long walks to talk to God and cry out.

My Bible became my pillow—literally.

I had no one to talk to. No one knew my story. God didn't release me to speak on it. My husband couldn't deliver me. He didn't understand my trial. I soon realized it was me and God. I was determined to obey God!

Intercession in the Storm

There were days when I was so worn out, then someone would call with an urgent need for prayer or counseling. I would minister to my mother-in-law. I would leave work and go pray with her or bring her home with my husband and I. She honored me as her daughter-in-law and as a woman of God. She also said, "You brought healing to this family." It definitely didn't feel that way at the time.

Many nights I got out of bed to intercede in prayer for the very ones who were stabbing me in the heart. Holy Spirit said, *"Pray now, and you will be healed!"*

We had to move to accommodate our niece. My sister moved in to help alleviate some of the load. How was I assigned to pray for and minister to them in the midst of my pain?

Not fair!

The Breaking Point

My daughter felt displaced with the house bursting at the seams. She didn't want to be there. We didn't know how to give space or grace for one another's pain. She didn't sign up for this. I constantly stayed on my knees in prayer for her, crying out day and night for her wounded soul.

The ongoing spiritual warfare had quietly begun to take a toll on my psyche. I was in a fog. I thought I was just bearing my cross, but all the time I was carrying grief. I had literally lost my appetite and my laughter. I began to lose weight and my joy.

No one saw me. When I would get home from work, I would want to hop into bed and pull the covers over my head, but the Holy Spirit stopped me.

He spoke to me: *"Keep it moving."* But depression was calling me. I asked for prayer, but was often told, *"You're strong. You're going to be alright!"*

Picture Perfect

Holy Spirit taught me how to renew my mind against the enemy's attacks.

God knew me and had a blueprint of what my life would look like, but that beautiful picture on the box of a puzzle will never come together when the pieces are lost and scattered.

I had to do the hard work of recovering my broken spirit, shattered dreams, discarded relationships, and my tattered heart. I had to become the prophet of my own soul. I had to reach down into the valley and call forth every missing, broken, and dead thing in my life. I had to get myself together!

God was perfecting a women's deliverance ministry through my trials. The very thing Satan came to rip apart withstood the storm. God put us together.

Our marriage remained intact. We just celebrated our 20th anniversary with true joy!

When my mom woke me up those many years ago amidst the broken glass drama, she didn't hit me or yell. She simply said, "You knew better. Get up and find all of the broken glass. I'll deal with you later."

God also woke me from the fog and helped me regather the fragmented parts of my life.

I am now equipped to speak shalom over the lives of other fractured sisters as a friend, life coach, and minister of the gospel.

I see now that I wasn't built to break!

REFLECTIONS FOR YOUR JOURNEY

1. What "broken glass" moments in your life forced you to gather the pieces and start again?

2. How can you choose to see trials not as shame but as preparation for your purpose?

_____

_____

_____

_____

_____

_____

_____

_____

_____

_____

_____

_____

_____

_____

_____

_____

ABOUT THE AUTHOR

Rosalyn Courtney Richardson is an intercessor, poet, and published writer. She is an ordained pastor, wife, mother, and proud grandmother. She has worked in education and the public library system for over 30 years. She is a life coach, wellness advisor, and founder of Heart's Whisper Women's Ministry, dedicated to empowering women through healing, prayer, and restoration.

You may have been broken,
but you are not beyond repair.
You are a warrior, a
survivor, and a thriver.

DR. ANGELA ROBERSON

STRENGTH TO STAND

Resilience, Faith, and the Courage to Rise Again

By Dr. Angela Roberson

As women, we've faced our fair share of challenges. We've been pushed, pulled, and tested in ways that would break a lesser person. But we're not lesser. We're strong, resilient, and capable of overcoming even the darkest of times.

As the Bible says, *"I can do all this through him who gives me strength"* (Philippians 4:13).

For those who have suffered abuse, rejection, and heartache, I want you to know that you're not alone. Your pain is valid, and your story matters.

It's easy to get lost in the darkness, to feel like you're drowning in a sea of despair. But I want you to know that you're stronger than you think.

"For I know the plans I have for you," declares the Lord, "plans to prosper you and not to harm you, plans to give you hope and a future."

Jeremiah 29:11

Broken but Not Beyond Repair

You may have been broken, but you're not beyond repair. Your heart may have been shattered, but it can be mended. You've survived every difficult moment, every painful experience, and every heartbreaking loss. And that's something to be proud of.

"Praise be to the God and Father of our Lord Jesus Christ, the Father of compassion and the God of all comfort, who comforts us in all our troubles."
2 Corinthians 1:3-4

It's okay to acknowledge the pain, to feel the weight of it. But don't let it define you. You are more than your struggles, more than your scars. You are a warrior, a survivor, and a thriver.

"We are hard pressed on every side, but not crushed; perplexed, but not in despair; persecuted, but not abandoned; struck down, but not destroyed."
2 Corinthians 4:8-9

Strength in Suffering

Remember the times you've faced adversity and come out on top. Remember the strength you've found within yourself, the resilience that's carried you through. You may not feel like it right now, but you are capable of overcoming anything.

"We also glory in our sufferings, because we know that suffering produces perseverance; perseverance, character; and character, hope."
Romans 5:3-4

Don't compare your journey to someone else's. Your path is unique, and your struggles are valid. Don't let anyone make you feel like you're not enough or that you've failed. You haven't failed. You've learned, grown, and survived.

"And we know that in all things God works for the good of those who love him, who have been called according to his purpose."
Romans 8:28

You Are Not Alone

You are not alone in this journey. There are people who care about you, who want to support you, and who believe in you. Reach out to them, lean on them, and let them help you through the tough times.

"Carry each other's burdens, and in this way you will fulfill the law of Christ."
Galatians 6:2

Your story is not over yet. There are still chapters to be written, still lessons to be learned, and still triumphs to be celebrated. Don't give up on yourself, even when it feels like the world is against you.

"And let us not grow weary of doing good, for in due season we will reap, if we do not give up."
Galatians 6:9

Remember Who You Are

You are strong, capable, and worthy of love and respect. You deserve to be treated with kindness, compassion, and dignity. Remember that, no matter what anyone else says or does.

"You are the light of the world. A town built on a hill cannot be hidden."
Matthew 5:14

As you move forward, remember to be gentle with yourself. Take time to heal, to rest, and to recharge. You're not a machine; you're a human being with feelings, needs, and desires.

"Come to me, all you who are weary and burdened, and I will give you rest"
Matthew 11:28

Celebrate your victories, no matter how small they may seem. Celebrate your strength, your resilience, and your courage. You are a warrior, and warriors deserve to celebrate their wins.

"Rejoice in the Lord always. I will say it again: Rejoice!"
Philippians 4:4

Standing Together

I still stand, and so do you. We stand together, side by side, as women who have faced adversity and come out on top.

We stand as warriors, as survivors, and as thrivers. We stand as testimonies to the human spirit, to the power of resilience, and to the strength of the human heart.

REFLECTIONS FOR YOUR JOURNEY

1. What past challenge nearly broke you, but instead became proof of your strength and resilience?
2. How can you remind yourself daily that your scars are not your definition, but your testimony?

_____

_____

_____

_____

_____

_____

_____

_____

_____

_____

_____

_____

_____

_____

_____

_____

_____

ABOUT THE AUTHOR

Apostle Dr. Angela Roberson is a dedicated humanitarian, educator, and accomplished author. She holds a bachelor's degree in biblical study and counseling and an honorary Doctorate of Divinity. She is a former licensed cardiac technician at Harbor UCLA Medical Centre, and founder and CEO of Heart 2 Heart Ministries International Foundation and Daughter of the King TV International Network, expanding ministry work to Africa, Jamaica, Mexico, and the Bahamas. Angela's books and television shows inspire worldwide audiences. Her mentorship programs in Compton and Johannesburg empower youth, reflecting her commitment to education, faith, and global outreach.

My scars are not signs of shame; they are reminders of survival, faith, and divine restoration.

◆―――――――◆

PROPHETESS LAKESHIA WALLACE

FROM PAIN TO PURPOSE

Surviving Emotional Abuse and Rising into Victory

By Prophetess Lakeshia Wallace

Have you ever been torn down with words? Constantly devalued and criticized by someone you love? That is emotional abuse, a pattern of insults, humiliation, and control that wears down your self-worth, confidence, and mental strength.

It can happen in relationships, friendships, family, or even at work, but often, it starts in a romantic relationship.

A well-dressed woman with a confident smile but eyes filled with sorrow hid behind a mask. My struggle began in my adolescent years with low self-esteem and a desperate search for love and validation in the arms of men. What I thought was love was really a search for worth.

This particular relationship began with romance and grand gestures. The kind of relationship that makes friends jealous. Gifts, roses, and expensive outings made me feel seen and cherished. Life was great. We were in love. I was his Bonnie, and he was my Clyde. Nothing or nobody could separate us.

At first, it was perfect. I mean everything was constant, but slowly, everything began to shift. Small comments turned into controlling words: *You think you're all that? You're nothing! Why are you wearing that? Don't talk to them!*

Before long, his words dictated how I dressed, where I went, and who I could see.

Isolation followed. I felt trapped, like a bird with clipped wings. Constantly anxious, walking on eggshells. He made others turn on me, painting me as crazy. And fed me lies about what others said about me.

Even going to church became a source of accusation. Then came betrayal. Whenever he cheated, the blame shifted to me as he would scream at the top of his lungs, "You're so jealous and insecure!"

The secrets I shared, the fears I whispered, the deepest parts of me I trusted him with—he turned them into weapons. And over time, I became mentally and physically ill. Trembling on the inside. Panic attacks left me gasping for help; my body felt chemically unbalanced.

The ambulance was called more times than I can count. I was a total wreck. My lifelines were my therapist, psychologist, and doctor. Overwhelmed by fear and shame, I didn't know how I could survive another day.

The Divine Shift

The turning point came one day while visiting my daughter. A whisper in my mind told me to jump from the eighth-floor window. Fear gripped me like never before, and I fell to my knees, crying out to God, "Lord, please save me. Don't let me lose my mind."

In that moment, I felt His presence: I was not alone. He gave me the strength to get up. I began seeking resources, stepping out on faith with no funds and only one bag, and found a safe home for women victims of abuse.

Counseling, workshops, and support helped me rebuild boundaries and self-worth. Through this journey, I joined an amazing church (The Wrecking Crew for Christ Holiness Church), prayed daily, and read the Bible, finding strength, peace, and clarity.

I met a beautiful woman of God, Keichelle Hampton, who prayed with me daily as I worked through withdrawals and trauma. Slowly, freedom and healing replaced fear. God's presence was evident in every step.

Forgiveness was the hardest part, but it was essential. I had to release forgiveness to receive God's healing. God softened my heart, and I realized the triumph was not just mine; it was His. And by trusting Him, healing became possible.

Standing in Victory

What was meant to destroy me became the very thing that strengthened me. My victory didn't come overnight; it came through prayer, perseverance, and trusting God in the hardest moments.

Every tear, every sleepless night, every fear I faced became a step toward freedom and healing.

I learned that overcoming is not measured by how quickly you leave a difficult season but by the courage it takes to rise when your heart feels shattered. Triumph is standing up even when you don't feel whole, knowing that God's power can restore what was broken.

I triumphed because God gave me strength when I had none left and hope when the darkness seemed endless.

I rose because I turned back to God. Abuse tried to silence me, but prayer gave me my voice again. His Word became my anchor, His presence my safe place.

Through forgiveness, I found freedom. Through worship, I found healing. And through faith, I found strength. I didn't rise by myself—God lifted me every step of the way.

Scriptures that once felt distant now spoke directly to my wounds, such as, *"He heals the brokenhearted and binds up their wounds"* (Psalm 147:3).

I started to understand that healing is not just physical or emotional; it is spiritual.

Today, I stand as living proof that what was meant to destroy me only pushed me closer to Him. I learned that pain does not define me. Purpose does. Forgiveness is not weakness, but freedom. Prayer changes not only circumstances but hearts. God can take the deepest wounds and turn them into testimonies of healing.

My story has power beyond my own understanding. My experiences, though painful, have given me insight, empathy, and a platform to help others.

Most of all, I am stronger, wiser, and whole in Him. My scars are not signs of shame; they are reminders of survival, faith, and divine restoration.

I am still standing because God is my strength. His grace carried me when I couldn't carry myself. His Spirit held me together when life tried to tear me apart.

I am still standing because His Word reminds me daily that I am more than a conqueror. Prayer keeps me grounded, and His love keeps me lifted.

But I'm not standing just for myself—I'm standing so others can rise, too. God turned my pain into purpose, and now I minister and advocate for women who feel broken, silenced, or forgotten. My testimony has become my ministry, and my scars are proof of His healing power.

I am not standing on my own. I am standing on Christ, the solid rock. And as long as I stand, I will help others rise.

From My Heart to Yours

To anyone reading this: maybe you've been silenced, belittled, or made to feel worthless. Hear me clearly, you are not defined by the abuse you endured.

You are not the cruel words spoken against you. What happened to you was real, but it does not diminish your value or strength. And you have the power to rise.

If I can rise, you can rise. If I can heal, you can heal. Your past may have shaped you, but it does not define your future. Healing takes time, but it is possible.

You are worthy of love, respect, and joy. You are more precious than rubies (Proverbs 3:15). Your story matters. Your voice matters.

God is turning your pain into your purpose. *"For I know the plans I have for you,"* declares the Lord, *"plans to prosper you and not to harm you, plans to give you hope and a future"* (Jeremiah 29:11).

REFLECTIONS FOR YOUR JOURNEY

1. What lies or cruel words spoken over you need to be released so you can walk in freedom?

2. How can you turn one area of pain in your life into purpose by helping others?

_____

_____

_____

_____

_____

_____

_____

_____

_____

_____

_____

_____

_____

_____

_____

_____

ABOUT THE AUTHOR

Prophetess Lakeshia Wallace is a prophetic voice with a heart for God's people. With over eight years in ministry, she empowers women through spiritual guidance, healing, and mentorship. A devoted mother and grandmother, she balances family with her calling. Married to Pastor Tony Wallace, they uphold a strong covenant in life and ministry. Over the last decade, she has been deeply involved in outreach, assisted ministry leaders, supported major conferences, and spoken at conferences, sharing her testimony and insights. She leads **HER Victory**, a ministry dedicated to healing, empowering, and restoring women, helping them embrace their value, voice, and victory in Christ.

Books by Strive Publishing

WWW.STRIVEIPG.COM